Drama

Steck Vaughn™

HOUGHTON MIFFLIN HARCOURT
Supplemental Publishers

www.SteckVaughn.com
800-531-5015

Drama

contents

Drama
Fact Matters

ISBN-13: 978-1-4190-5449-5
ISBN-10: 1-4190-5449-X

First published by Blake Education Pty Ltd as *Go Facts*
Copyright © 2006 Blake Publishing
This edition copyright under license from Blake Education Pty Ltd
© 2010 Steck-Vaughn, an imprint of HMH Supplemental Publishers Inc.

Steck-Vaughn is a trademark of HMH Supplemental Publishers Inc.

Printed in China

1 2 3 4 5 6 7 8   373   15 14 13 12 11 10 09 08

What Is Drama?

*Drama is acting out a story in front of an **audience**.*

The story is called a play. It is **performed** by actors. Some plays are about real people. Others are made-up. The actors might speak or be silent. They might also sing and dance.

Actors learn their lines. Lines are what actors have to say in a play. The actors practice the play together. This is called a **rehearsal**.

Everyone practices until the play is perfect. The play is then performed for an audience. A play can be performed in a theater or in front of a camera. Some plays are even shown in parks.

Drama can entertain you. It can make you feel strong emotions. It can also teach you about how people deal with problems.

Acting classes teach people to act.

The **director** decides how the play should be.

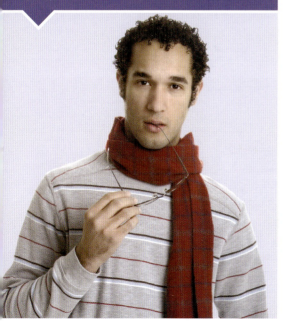

Drama often contains a lot of action and excitement.

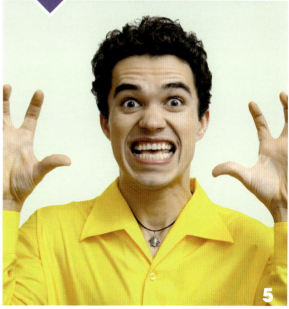

5

Ancient Greek Drama

Modern Western theater began with the ancient Greeks.

Theater was first performed in Greece some time before 534 B.C.E. in Athens. The earliest recorded author was a man named Thespis. It is from his name that we get the term **thespian**.

Early Greek plays used a **chorus** to help tell the story. The chorus would explain things to the audience. It would explain background information or what a character was feeling.

The ancient Greeks created different types of plays. One type is **tragedy**. Tragedies are usually very serious plays with sad endings. The other type is **comedy**. Comedies are meant to make the audience laugh.

These images are a mask of comedy and a mask of tragedy.

Sophocles was a famous writer of Greek tragedies.

Did You Know?

Before Greek theater started, drama was performed in India and China. This was more than 3,500 years ago.

Plays were performed in this ancient theater in Athens.

Reading a Play

*The **script** is the story of the play.*

A play's script is mostly the lines spoken by the characters. Many scripts also include **descriptions** of the characters. They may also have descriptions of the **setting** and what action is happening.

Most plays are broken up into **acts**. Plays usually have one to five acts. The acts are often broken up into **scenes**. There is a description of the characters and setting before or during a scene. There may also be **stage directions**. These explain what the actors should do. The stage directions also explain how actors should read their lines.

The script has everything an actor needs to know to perform the play.

These actors are in costume.

This woman is performing on stage.

Preparing to Perform

*Here is how to **prepare** for a stage play:*

1. Actors **audition** for the roles. They must do a short performance to show their acting skills. The director chooses and hires the best actors.

2. A stage crew is hired. The stage crew builds **sets** and makes costumes.

3. The actors memorize their scripts. They practice their lines and how they will move on stage.

4. The play is ready to be performed. The first performance for an audience is called opening night.

On the Stage

Actors perform on a stage in a theater.

The audience sits in rows in front of the stage. Actors move on and off the stage from its **wings**, or sides. The sides and back of the stage are hidden from the audience. A curtain hangs in front of the stage. When it is lowered, the audience cannot see the stage.

A lowered curtain shows that a scene has ended. When it is raised, a new scene begins. Many plays have more than one setting. This means that different **props** and backgrounds need to be on the stage at different times. These quick setting changes are made while the curtain is down.

A stage doesn't have to be inside a theater.

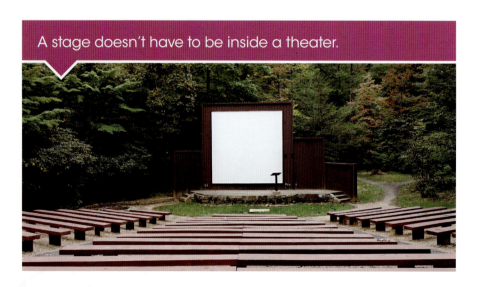

curtain

wing

wing

up stage

stage right

down stage

stage left

This woman is making sure the costume is ready.

KEEP AWAY
AUTHORIZED
OPERATORS
ONLY

The backstage area is where props are stored.

The Greatest Playwright

*William Shakespeare wrote plays more than 400 years ago. Many consider him to be the greatest **playwright** of all time.*

Shakespeare was born in England in 1564. He wrote 38 plays that we know of. His plays have been translated into almost every language. Shakespeare wrote both tragedies and comedies.

One of Shakespeare's most famous plays is the tragedy *Romeo and Juliet.* It is the story of a young man and woman, Romeo and Juliet, who fall in love. However, their families are enemies. Romeo and Juliet try to be together. But they face many problems.

There have been many **interpretations** of *Romeo and Juliet.* An interpretation is the way the play is presented. Usually the basic story remains the same, but the setting or words may change.

Did You Know?

More films have been made based on William Shakespeare's plays than those of any other writer.

Romeo and Juliet dance in a ballet interpretation of the play.

Many of Shakespeare's plays were performed at the Globe Theater.

Different Kinds of Acting

People don't just act on stage.

People act in front of cameras, too. This type of acting happens in movies or on television shows. Acting in front of a camera is different from acting on a stage.

People who act on stage have to speak loudly. Their voices must reach everyone in the audience. But actors in front of a camera don't have to worry about that. They can talk at a normal volume. They can even whisper.

An actor might make a mistake in front of the camera. The scene can be filmed again. But if an actor makes a mistake on stage, it can't be undone. The play must go on.

This actor is rehearsing.

When the curtain opens, the play will begin.

This video camera is used to record actors.

Here is an old camera that was used to film movies.

Acting Without a Script

Actors have scripts that tell them what to say in a play. What happens when there isn't a script?

Improvisation is drama where actors make up the words as they act. The actors know the idea behind each scene. They create the story and words for the scene. Sometimes the actors ask the audience what should happen next. Most improvisation is meant to be funny.

Improvisation is often taught in acting classes. Improvisation requires important acting skills. It teaches actors how to work together and listen to each other.

Actors play improvisation games. The funniest team wins!

Did You Know?

Actors warm up their voices by speaking out loud. Say the following tongue twister three times to warm up your voice:

"A big black bug bit a big black bear."

In improvisation you do not know what will happen next on stage.

Music and Drama

The ancient Greeks had music and dancing in their plays. We still have music and dance in our drama today.

Opera is drama in which the actors sing their lines. Opera began in Italy in the late 16th century. Operas often have **elaborate** costumes and sets. Operas are usually performed in the language they were written in. This means that audiences may not understand the words being sung.

A musical is drama that has singing and dancing as well as dialogue. Musicals are very popular. They are performed around the world. A well-known **composer** of musicals is Sir Andrew Lloyd Webber. One of his most famous musicals is called *Cats*.

Opera singers use music to show feelings and emotions.

These actors are dancing on stage.

Many musicals are performed on Broadway, a group of famous theaters in New York City.

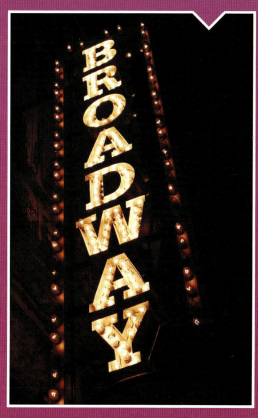

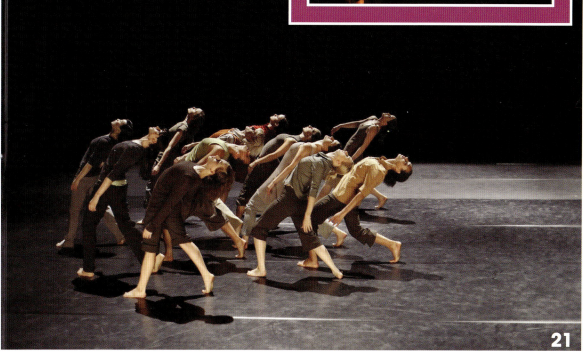

What Actors Do

	Speak	Sing	Dance	Rehearse	
An opera	no	yes	maybe	yes	
A play	yes	no	no	yes	
A musical	yes	yes	yes	yes	
An improvisation	yes	maybe	maybe	no	

Glossary

acts (aktz) the divisions of a play or opera

audience (AH dee uhns) the people watching a performance

audition (ah DIH shuhn) a short performance by an actor to try to get a part in a play

chorus (KOR uhs) a group of actors who explain the action in a play

comedy (KAH muh dee) a play that is meant to be funny

composer (kuhm POH zuhr) someone who writes music

description (dih SKRIHP shuhn) a composition or account that gives a picture in words

director (duhr EHK tuhr) the person in charge of a play

elaborate (eh LA bor uht) having a lot of detail

improvisation (ihm prah vih ZAY shuhn) a scene in which the words and actions are made up by the actors as they go

interpretation (ihn ter pruh TAY shuhn) an idea of how a story should be told

perform (pruh FORM) to put on a play; to act

playwright (PLAY ryt) someone who writes plays

prepare (prih PAIR) to get ready

props (prahps) objects used by actors on stage

rehearsal (ree HUR suhl) a practice performance of a play

scenes (seenz) the divisions within the acts of a play or opera

script (skrihpt) the words the actors say in a play

set (seht) the scenery and props in a play

setting (SEH tihng) where something takes place

stage directions (stayj duh REHK shuhnz) directions given in a play to the actors and director

thespian (THEHS pee uhn) an actor

tragedy (TRA juh dee) a play meant to be serious; has a sad ending

wings (weengz) the sides of the stage that the audience cannot see

Index